Say No
To
Bullying

Sebreana Plunkett

Copyright © 2019 Sebreana Plunkett

All rights reserved.

ISBN: 9798860820661

DEDICATION
I WOULD LIKE TO DEDICATE THIS BOOK TO MY LOVING AND SUPPORTIVE FAMILY

Pg3

TABLE OF CONTENTS

TABLE OF CONTENTS

1 Peter 4:8 Above all, love each other deeply, because love covers over a multitude of sins.

Pg6

UNITED WE STAND

United We Stand means despite one's gender, race, ethnicity

or status , we all in God's eyes are one. It doesn't matter

who you are , or what you may or may not have, you too

will be held accountable for your

actions against another.

Pg7

ACKNOWLEDGMENTS

To my wonderful family, children, and grandchildren who inspire me to help others and give back.

Pg8

Love Yourself & Others. Treat others the way you want to be treated.

What is your definition of bullying?

1. _____
2. _____
3. _____

Bullying affects someone in many ways.
Describe how bullying made you feel.

1. _____
2. _____
3. _____

CHAPTER 1 COURAGEOUS

YOU ARE COURAGEOUS FOR STANDING UP TO A

BULLY AND TELLING SOMEONE.

Pg11

EXPRESSIONS OF LOVE

What are some ways you express love for self and others?

1. _____

2. _____

3. _____

Pg12

CHAPTER 2 BE KIND

BE KIND AND TREAT OTHERS WITH RESPECT

Pg13

CHAPTER 3 TELL SOMEONE

IF SOMEONE IS BULLYING YOU OR BULLYING SOMEONE YOU KNOW, MAKE SURE YOU TELL SOMEONE . TELL AS MANY PEOPLE YOU TO.

Rise up,
take
courage,
and do it.

TELL SOMEONE

Teachers are there to help you, protect you and guide you.

Don't be afraid to report bullying.

Pg15

CHAPTER 4 LISTEN

CAREFULLY LISTEN TO OTHERS WHEN THEY

ATTEMPT TO SHARE THEIR FEELINGS WITH YOU.

PG16

Your bravery & courage could save life's or even someone

who's considering committing suicide or causing potential danger to self and others.

Pg17

CHAPTER 5 LOVE THY NEIGHBOR

Love thy neighbor means loving an individual without

prejudice and judgement. Love your friends, family and

classmates. Respect ones preferences.

Pg18

CHAPTER 6 BULLYING

BULLYING AFFECTS YOU PSYCHOLOGICALLY, EMOTIONALLY, SOCIALLY AND PHYSICALLY.

CHAPTER 7 SIGNS OF BEING BULLIED

NOT EATING

NOT BEING SOCIABLE

NOT ENGAGING WITH FAMILY

BEING DISTANT

UNEXPLAINED INJURIES

LOST OR DESTROYED CLOTHING

FAKING SICKNESS

DECLINING GRADES

CHAPTER 8 PEER PRESSURE

DON'T BE AFRAID TO SPEAK UP AND DISTANCE YOURSELF FROM PEOPLE THAT DO NOT TREAT OTHERS INCLUDING YOURSELF WITH RESPECT AND DIGNITY. DO NOT ALLOW OTHERS TO PERSUADE YOU INTO DOING THINGS UNGODLY AND UNJUSTIFIED.

CHAPTER 9 CHANGING CIRCLE'S

IF SOMEONE IS MISTREATING YOU AND YOU'RE

NOT SURE WHAT TO DO?, IMMEDIATELY

REMOVE YOURSELF FROM THAT CIRCLE AND

FIND YOU SOME BETTER FRIENDS.

Pg22

CHAPTER 10 BE OBSERVANT

TAKE NOTICE OF OTHERS BEHAVIOR IN THE

CLASSROOM OR WORK SPACE AND REPORT THE

CONCERN .

Pg23

Smile because you did something courageous today.

Note what action was taken:

1. _____
2. _____
3. _____

Smile because you helped someone who couldn't help themselves.

Note what actions was taken:

1. _____
2. _____
3. _____

You're amazing!! You changed someone's life today.

Pg25

أجمل النساء من تزور
الناس دون أطفالها ـ
ـ نزار قباني

"أطفال عرب دون أمنية"

Continue observing, listening and taking notes of unusual

behaviors.

Pg26

Chapter 11 Commitment

Be ~ committed to making the right decisions .

Be ~ committed to looking after others' well being.

Be ~ committed to protecting your friends, family and classmates.

Be ~ committed to having sympathy for the discouraged, sad and weak.

Pg27

CHAPTER 12 Being Brave

Being brave means to stand up to anyone regardless of size, gender and age. Never be intimidated by a bully.

Bullied are people who lack self love and enjoy seeing others hurt.

ABOUT THE AUTHOR

Sebreana is a Savannah, Ga native who attended Chatham County public schools. Later enrolling at Savannah Technical College where she furthered her education. Sebreana went on working in the healthcare industry serving over 23 years with grace and compassion. This extraordinary individual loves helping others and spending time with her family.

Pg29

If you see something, say something.

Pg30

If you see something, say something.

Pg31

Bullying is not acceptable or tolerated.

Pg32

IT'S ENOUGH!

Have you ever experienced or witnessed bullying in your

school?

Yes _____

No _____

If yes, Did you tell someone?

Yes _____

No _____

Pg33

IT'S ENOUGH!

Did the bullying seized?

Yes _____

No _____

Do you feel you did the right thing by reporting this

behavior?

Yes _____

No

SAVE SOMEONE FROM BEING BULLIED OR HARASSED

Pg35

SAVE YOURSELF FROM BEING BULLIED OR HARASSED

Pg36

How do you feel about someone being bullied?

_____

_____

_____

_____

_____

_____

_____

Pg37

1 Peter 4:8

Above all, love each other deeply, because love covers a

 multiple of sins.

Pg38

Love yourself & Love others!

Made in the USA
Columbia, SC
20 November 2023

26531508R00022